A Taste of Peru

The Best Peruvian Recipes

by
Daniel McKay

A Taste of Peru. The Best Peruvian Recipes.

Version 2012.11.04

Print Edition 1.1

ISBN : 978-1480248106

MAIN DISHES 43

Lomo Saltado 44

Aji de Gallina 47

Seco de Res 50

Tacu Tacu 53

Arroz con Pato 56

Pollo a la Brasa 59

Chicharrones 61

Octopus in Olive Sauce 63

Pescado Sudado 65

Causa de Pollo 67

Goat Stew 71

Pot Roast 73

Fish Ceviche 75

Scallop Ceviche 77

DESSERTS 79

Tres Leches 80

Picarones with Syrup 83

Sweet Potato Flan 87

DRINKS 89

Dedication

This dedication is to all those who have helped me with this book and given advice on the recipes. I hope you all get to enjoy a taste or Peru.

Introduction

Peruvian food is world renowned for its high quality and incredible variety of dishes. Peruvian cuisine draws upon many influences and hence there is such a wide range of wonderful dishes. Influences come from countries such as Italy, Spain, Japan, China and West Africa.

Throughout Peru there is a huge diversity of cuisine, ranging from the coastal cuisine, dominated by sea food dishes, to the Andean highland cuisine which is a little heartier and based more on potato, rice and meat dishes, to the jungle cuisine which contains yuccas and banana based fruit.

After spending sometime in Peru learning about the culture I felt it only fitting to share some of the best Peruvian recipes so you can try these delicious dishes at home. In some cases getting the exact ingredients may be tricky, but there are some simple substitutes that will allow you to make the most authentic dish possible with the ingredients you have to available, without compromising the integrity of the dish.

As an added bonus I have included some of the most famous drinks at the end of the book. What Peruvian meal would be complete without Chicha Morada or a Pisco Sour? In my opinion none, hence the small drinks section at the end of the book.

An important note: this book is by no means a complete list of recipes from Peru, we would need a library for all of those. Yet, this book is a selection of some of the best dishes, soups, starters and drinks from Peru providing you the opportunity to experience some Incan deliciousness in your own kitchen.

I hope you enjoy these dishes as much as I have enjoyed them. Peruvian cuisine really is one of the culinary wonders of the world. One of the really great things about Peruvian cuisine is that there is something for every ones taste.

Sizing and Abbreviation

It makes sense that we just clarify the sizing and abbreviation used in this recipe book. Firstly, all of the recipes in this book are quoted first in imperial units with metric units in brackets.

Cup size can sometimes feel a bit ambiguous, so whenever a cup is referred to we are assuming a cup equals to 8 fluid ounces, which is approximately 227 ml.

A tablespoon, which has the abbreviation tbsp. in this book, is equal to half a fluid ounce, which equates to approximately 14 ml.

A teaspoon, which has the abbreviation tsp. in this book, is one sixth of a fluid ounce, which equates to approximately 5 ml.

All other abbreviations are standard, for example oz. for ounce, Kg for Kilogram.

Soups

Here we have three fantastic recipes for soups, each has a different style and all are worth the time to make and try. I hope you enjoy them all.

Peruvian Creole Soup

This is a classic Peruvian soup, or as it is called in Spanish 'Sopa a la Criolla'. This makes a great winter warmer. This is a rich orange colored beef soup, which almost looks like an Asian noodle soup. The chili's, add a little bit of kick to the soup and if you are a fan of spicy food you can increase the amount of chili's to suit you palate. Note, the aji chili is the Peruvian hot chili pepper. If you are unable to get hold of the aji chili then either the Habanero or Serrano chili will make a suitable replacement.

Ingredients for 4 good servings

- 1 lb. (0.5Kg) Beef

- 1 Large onion

- 5 Tomatoes

- 4 Garlic cloves

- 8 Cups of beef stock

- 2 Sun dried yellow aji chili's.

- 4 Large eggs

- 2 tbsp. of tomato paste

- 3 oz. of angel hair pasta

- Half a cup of evaporated milk

- Vegetable Oil

- Salt, Pepper and Oregano.

Preparation - 45 mins

1. Finely chop the onion, tomatoes and crush the garlic gloves.

2. Chop the beef up into small bite size portions and season with a little salt and pepper.

3. Heat some vegetable oil in the bottom of a deep skillet and add the seasoned beef and cook for a couple of minutes. This is just to seal the meat.

4. Add the finely chopped onion and crushed garlic into the skillet with the beef. Cook until the onion is slightly brown, but not caramelized.

5. Add the tomatoes along with the yellow aji chili into the skillet. Continue to cook at a medium heat until the majority of the liquid has evaporated.

6. Add in the tomato paste, give this a stir and then straight away add the 8 cups of beef stock.

7. Now with all beef stock added bring the heat up so that the soup begins to boil. At this point you can then add the pasta and maintain the heat until the pasta is completely cooked. This will take around 5 to 10 minutes depending on how soft or hard you like your pasta.

8. When the pasta is cooked you can reduce the heat to a steady simmer and add the milk and

stir it into the soup.

9. Poach the eggs, separate from the main pot.

10. The soup is now ready to be served. Add one poached egg to each bowl and then sprinkle some oregano on top of the soup.

Peruvian Chicken Soup

Locally this soup is called Aguadito de Pollo. The soup has a greenish color, which makes it kind of look like a chicken and vegetable pea soup, but it's far nicer. This hearty soup can easily replace a meal or be served as a starter. Note, if you are unable to get hold of aji chili paste you can try cayenne paste or Tabasco paste as a replacement.

Ingredients for 4 good servings

- 6 Chicken drumsticks or thighs, or a mix of both.

- 1 Large Onion

- 1 Carrot

- 1 Bunch cilantro

- 2 Cloves of garlic

- 1 tbsp. of aji chili paste

- 1 tsp. of Cumin

- 3 Large potatoes

- Half a cup of virgin olive oil

- 10 Cups of Chicken Broth

- 1 Cup of white rice

- Salt and Pepper

Preparation - 45 to 60 minutes

1. Use a large heavy pot and place it on a medium heat with the olive oil in the bottom of the pot.

2. Finely chop the onion, cut the carrot into cubes, cut the potatoes into quarters, crush the garlic cloves and finely chop up the cilantro.

3. Add to the pot the finely chopped onion, the crushed garlic and the aji chili to the hot oil. Cook for 1 to 2 minutes until the onions have softened.

4. It is optional if you would like to add some seasoning with the salt and pepper to the chicken before adding it to the pot.

5. Add the chicken to the pot and cook to seal the chicken. This will take at least 5 minutes.

6. Add the finely chopped cilantro and stir for a further minute or two.

7. Add all the remaining ingredients to the pot. The 10 cups of chicken broth, the 3 large chopped potatoes, the chopped carrot, the rice and the cumin.

8. Bring this all to the boil, stirring occasionally, then, reduce the heat until simmering. Continue with a simmer until everything is cooked. The potatoes should be soft and tender and the chicken should be cooked all the way through.

9.   It is now ready to be served, be sure to include at least one piece of chicken in each soup bowl.

Fish Soup Peruvian Style

No book on Peruvian cuisine would be complete without at least one fish soup recipe, and this one is a good one. Because of the number of ingredients required this makes a larger quantity than normal. The following with will give you 6 very good portions and with a little more fish fillet, an extra half or even one pound and this will stretch easily to 8 servings. Note, if you cannot get hold of an aji chili either a Serrano or Habanero can be used as a replacement.

Ingredients for 6 good servings

- 1 lb. (0.5 Kg) Cod fillet

- 0.5 lb. (0.25 Kg) Scallops

- 0.5 lb. (0.25 Kg) Squid

- 14 oz. (0.4 kg) Tomatoes

- 8 oz. (227 ml) Clam juice

- 1 tbsp. Vegetable oil

- 1 Onion

- 1 aji chili

- 2 Garlic cloves

- 1 tsp. Cumin

that may exist.

2.   Use a bowl to mix together the pepper, the cumin, the chili leaves, the oregano, the salt, the garlic and the vinegar. This creates your marinate for the meat.

3.   Place the meat into the marinade, make sure the heart is completely covered and leave to rest for at least 3 hours.

4.   The now marinated heart is ready to be place onto skewers, and I would recommend you stick with Peruvian convention here and place three pieces of heart per skewer.

5.   In the left over marinade add some oil, virgin olive oil works pretty well. This is needed for the heart when it is placed on the grill.

6.   With the BBQ grill now nice and hot, wet the skewers and heart in the left over marinade and place the skewers on the grill. Every time you rotate the skewers be sure to paste them with some of the remaining marinade. Be careful not to burn the meat.

7.   Serve 2 skewers per person directly on a plate with French fries, leaving the meat on the skewers.

Stuffed Avocado

These make the ideal healthy starter. You can reduce the amount of potato and add some small shrimps or tuna in its place and this makes a great variation of the dish.

Ingredients for 4 servings

- 2 Large Avocados
- The juice of one lemon
- 1 Potato
- 1 piece of Celery
- 1 Carrot
- 2 Eggs
- Half a cup of peas
- Half a cup of Mayonnaise
- Salt and pepper

Preparation - 25 minutes

1. Cut the Potato up into small chunks and par boil.

2. At the same time in a different saucepan cut the

carrot up into small chunks also and cook until it is soft.

3. Next step, or even better if you can do it at the same time is to hard-boil the eggs.

4. Note, if you are using frozen peas, which is most likely the case, then you will also need to cook these. Use the microwave for these, place the peas in a container with some water in the bottom and pop in the microwave for 1 to 2 minutes and they are ready to go.

5. Cut the avocados in half, from top to bottom so that you have two identical halves. Then remove the seeds and peal the skin from the avocados.

6. In a bowl, mix the cooked potato, the chopped up carrot, the cooked peas and the mayonnaise. Add a pinch of salt to this mixture.

7. This mixture can now be spooned into the avocado halves. And to finish off, cut the hard boiled eggs into halves and place one half on the top of each stuffed avocado.

Papa a la Huancaina

This is truly a classic Peruvian dish, a mild spicy creamy sauce over boiled potatoes and lettuce. It is far more appetizing that it sounds. Papa a la Huancaina is an easy dish to prepare and a great addition to some of those BBQ's.

Ingredients for 4 servings

- 4 Large Potatoes
- 12 oz. (340 grams) Soft white cheese
- 1 Egg
- Half a cup Vegetable oil
- 6 oz. (170 ml) can of evaporated milk
- 2 Olives
- 4 Lettuce leaves
- 8 Crackers (non salty)
- A pinch of yellow aji chili (or cayenne)
- Salt

Preparation - 2 hours

1. Bring a pan of water to the boil and place both

the potatoes and the egg in and boil together.

2.   When the potatoes are cooked remove them and the egg from the pan, and peel the potatoes and remove he shell from the egg.

3.   Using a blender, mix half of the oil and all of the chili until you have a paste. Add more oil if necessary.

4.   Next add the cheese and the can of evaporated milk to the blender and continue until you have a consistent mixture.

5.   To thicken the mixture, break up some of the crackers and add to the blender and mix.

6.   This is the Huancaina sauce. Leave this sauce mixture sit for 30 minutes.

7.   Cut the potatoes into thick slices.

8.   Put a lettuce leaf on each plate, placing the potato on top of the lettuce.

9.   Now pour the sauce evenly over the potato, and garnish with both the olives, which need to be cut into quarters, and with a quarter egg on each plate. Bingo, there you have Papa a la Huancaina, which is served chilled. You can place the plates in the fridge for an hour or two whilst you prepare other dishes.

Mango Curry Ceviche

This is a tasty and colorful ceviche dish, which draws on the sweet flavor of the Mango. It is a great simple dish with which to impress friends.

Ingredients for 4 servings

- 1 lb. (0.5Kg) halibut or flounder
- Half a mango
- 1 Ají chili
- 1 Garlic
- 1 Onion
- Juice of 4 limes
- 1 tbsp. mango puree
- 1 tsp. curry
- 1 Celery stick
- Lettuce
- Salt

Preparation - 1 hour

1. Cut the fish (either halibut or flounder) into

very thin strips.

2.   Crush the garlic and mince the aji chili (note a habanero will make a suitable replacement if you cannot get hold of an aji).

3.   Thinly slice the mango and the onion.

4.   With the exception of the lettuce, place all the ingredients into a bowl and mix together thoroughly. Then leave the bowl in a refrigerator for at least 45 minutes before serving.

5.   Serve the ceviche onto a lettuce leaf placed on the plate and enjoy.

Grilled Corn

This is a nice simple one, which makes a great snack, starter or side dish. Note that if you cannot get hold of aji panca, then paprika will do just fine as a replacement.

Ingredients for 4 Servings

- 4 Fresh corn

- 6 oz. Butter

- 1 Cup Basil

- 2 tsp. Ají Panca

- Salt and Pepper

Preparation - 1 hour 15 minutes

1. Remove the silk from the corn but leave the husks in place.

2. Finely chop up the basil.

3. Now in a small bowl soften the butter and add in the aji panca or paprika, and the basil and mix all of this together with a spoon.

4. Without removing the husks, peal them back so that the mixture in the bowl can be spread around the corncob.

5.   Close the husks back up on the corn and wrap
       firmly with aluminium foil.

6.   Now leave on a grill with a medium heat for
       about one hour. You will need to turn the corn
       every 10 minutes.

7.   When the corn kernels are nice and soft the
       corn is ready to be served.

Quinoa Tabbouleh

This is a vegetarian dish which is very easy to make and very tasty. This can very easily be used as a side dish, or purely as a starter. Perfect for those warm summer days, and goes great with any BBQ.

Ingredients for 4 servings

- 2 cups quinoa
- 3 Tomatoes
- 1 Onion
- 1 Red pepper
- 1 cup parsley leaves
- 2 tbsp. fresh mint leaves
- 1 Garlic clove
- Half a tsp. basil
- Quarter cup of olive oil
- Quarter cup green olives
- Lemon juice
- Salt and Pepper

Preparation - 1 hour 30 minutes

1. Peel, seed and dice the tomatoes into very small chunks. Then very finely chop the onion up.

2. Mince the mint leaves, the basil and the parsley. Then crush the garlic.

3. Deseed the red pepper and cut into very small pieces.

4. Rinse the quinoa thoroughly, then drain and add to a pot of boiling water, and cook until it is soft. This will take approximately 15 minutes.

5. Now that the quinoa is cooked, you need to drain the water from the pot and leave to cool. It is best to put the quinoa in a bowl for this, as you will need a bowl to mix in the vegetables.

6. Add the chopped onion, tomatoes, mint, parsley, basil, garlic into the bowl with the quinoa. Mix this all together and season with the salt, pepper, lemon juice and olive oil.

7. Place this bowl into a refrigerator and leave for one hour. Then it is ready to serve. To garnish, add the chopped pepper and slice the olives.

Sauces / Salsas

Side sauces are so popular and important with Peruvian food that I had to make sure you get to try the most popular ones. These can be served with almost any dish, plate or soup. These sauces are also very good with just French fries.

Salsa Criolla

Salsa Criolla is a simple and quick salsa to prepare. It is a spicy onion based salsa, which makes a great accompaniment to a large number of dishes.

As with many other dishes in this book the aji pepper may not be available to you, but either the habanero or jalapeño make reasonable replacements.

Ingredients

*   2 Red onions

*   2 Ají chili peppers

*   1 tbsp. Cilantro

*   2 tbsp. Lime juice

*   1 tbsp. Vinegar

*   Salt and Pepper

Preparation - 45 minutes

1. Cut the 2 red onions into very thin half moon slices.

2. Slice the 2 aji peppers (if you cannot aji, habanero or jalapeño) into thin matchsticks, the thinner the better.

3.   While you have the cutting board out, chop up the cilantro very finely.

4.   Now with a bowl, add water and a few pinches of salt and soak the onions for 10 minutes. After 10 minutes drain and let dry the mixture.

5.   Now the vinegar, cilantro and lime juice can be added to the onion mixture. Give this all a good mix and then leave covered under plastic wrap at room temperature for at least 30 minutes before serving.

6.   Any of the salsa that is not used can be stored in a refrigerator for up to a couple of days.

Chimichurri Sauce

This is like a green relish sauce, very good with almost any dish. It is not at all spicy and I often eat this with French fries or even better on a piece of meat.

Ingredients

- 16 Garlic cloves

- 6 oz. (170 ml) Canola oil

- 1 cup minced parsley

- Third of a cup Oregano

- Half a small minced white onion

- 2 tbsp. of white vinegar

- 1 tsp. Sugar

- 1 tsp. pepper

- 1 tsp. salt

Preparation - 40 minutes

1. Mince the garlic cloves, mince the parsley, mince the fresh Oregano, finely chop up the half a white onion.

2. Next, using a bowl, add all of the ingredients

together and mix them well.

3. Now, cover and place for at 30 minutes in a refrigerator before serving.

Rocoto Sauce

This is the really hot sauce in Peru. It uses rocoto peppers and is very popular. However be forewarned that this is a hot red sauce. Here is a very quick way of making a simple rocoto sauce.

Ingredients

- 1 Rocoto pepper
- Half a cup of evaporated milk
- 6 tbsp. Lime juice
- 1 cup Olive oil
- 1 tsp. Salt
- Pepper

Preparation - 15 minutes

1. Wash the rocoto pepper thoroughly.

2. With caution, and it is wise to wear gloves and not to touch your face when handing the rocoto pepper, seed and cut the pepper into small pieces.

3. Using a blender, put in the cut pepper, the lime juice and the evaporated milk.

4.   Whilst blending, gradually add in the olive oil to create a creamy sauce.

5.   Add salt and pepper to taste.

6.   It is now ready to serve.

Aji Yellow Sauce

This is yet another hot sauce, and it goes with any dish.

Ingredients for half a cup

- 2 oz. (56 grams) of aji chili peppers

- A splash of Olive oil

- Half cup of Mayonnaise

- Half cup of Sour Cream

- Lime Juice

- Salt

Preparation - 1 hour

1. First you will need to create the paste, you could actually just buy this aji paste over the internet, but it is far more fun to make this fresh.

2. For the aji paste you need to cut open the aji peppers and remove the seeds and veins.

3. Place the peppers in a pot with water covering the peppers on the stove, bring to the boil and then simmer for half an hour.

4. Allow the peppers to cool a little, remove from the water and remove the skins.

5.   The remaining peppers then need to be place
        into a pan with hot oil and fry until lightly
        brown.

6.   These peppers can now be put in a blender and
        you have you aji paste.

7.   Now all the ingredients including the aji paste
        can be place into a bowl and whisked together.
        Add salt as desired.

8.   Your aji yellow sauce is ready for serving. Note,
        it can be conserved in the refrigerator for
        several days.

Main Dishes

Here is a varied selection of some truly awesome Peruvian recipes. I have included a mix of meat and seafood recipes and hopefully you will get the chance to enjoy all these. A little taste of Peru at home.

Lomo Saltado

What recipe book on Peruvian food could possibly be considered any good without a recipe for the simply awesome Lomo Saltado. This is basically beef stir-fry, Peru style, and it is delicious! This needs French fries as part of the dish and rice to accompany it with. Neither of these are covered in this recipe so bare that in mind when preparing this dish.

Ingredients for 4 good servings

- 1.5 lbs. (0.7 Kg) Beef tenderloin

- 3 tbsp. Oil

- 1 Red onion

- 3 Garlic cloves

- 2 Ají yellow chili's

- 3 Plum tomatoes

- Quarter cup of soy sauce

- 3 tbsp. Red wine vinegar

- Salt and pepper

- 1 lb. (0.45 Kg) French Fries

Preparation - 30 minutes

1. Very thinly slice the red onion and mince the 3 garlic cloves. Seed and cut the chili peppers and tomatoes into small strips.

2. Now, the beef needs to be cut into strips of approximately 2 inches long by a quarter inch thick. It is best to cut against the grain for the best results.

3. Using a wok or large frying pan heat some oil over a high heat.

4. Throw in the cut strips of beef and stir fry until cooked, but no more than a couple of minutes. Then remove the beef from the pan and set aside on a plate.

5. If needed add a little more oil to the wok or pan and heat on a high heat.

6. Throw in the finely chopped onion, the minced garlic, the chopped peppers and stir-fry until the onion is cooked but still retains some crunchiness. This will take around three minutes.

7. Next, in go the 3 chopped tomatoes, the quarter cup of soy sauce, the 3 tbsp. of red vinegar, a pinch of salt to taste. Stir fry all this for approximately one minute and then put the cooked beef back into the pan.

8. Add the cooked French fries to the pan or wok with everything else and heat through mixing it all together to make sure that the flavors mix well. Adjust to taste with salt and pepper. This

will only take a few minutes.

9.   Now, along with a portion of rice serve a large
       helping from the wok on each plate and there
       you have Lomo Saltado!

Aji de Gallina

Chili pepper chicken, this is a fantastic dish, which is like a mild curry. What is great is that the dish can also be used to fill pies or empanadas. One point to note is that this dish is best served with rice, and the preparation of rice is not dealt with in this recipe, so plan accordingly.

Ingredients for 4 servings

- 2 lbs. (0.9 Kg) Chicken breast
- 1 Onion
- 2 Garlic cloves
- 8 oz. Evaporated milk
- 3 tbsp. oil
- 2 Ají chili peppers
- 1 cup Fresh bread crumbs
- Half cup of ground Walnuts
- Half cup of grated Parmesan
- Salt and pepper

Preparation - 1 hour 15 minutes

1. Finely chop the onion, mince the 2 garlic cloves and finely cut up the 2 aji chili peppers.

2. Using a large pot, fill it with water and place the chicken in and bring to the boil. Note, that the chicken should be skinless and boneless before putting into the pot.

3. When you have achieved a boil, reduce the heat and allow to simmer for at least half an hour until the chicken is tender and fully cooked.

4. Now, carefully remove the chicken from the pot, but leaving the water in the pot. Leave the chicken to cool enough so that you can shred it apart in your hands into small pieces.

5. Put some oil into another large pan and heat on medium-high. Now, add the finely chopped onion, peppers and garlic and saute for 4 or 5 minutes until the onions are translucent.

6. Now the shredded chicken can be added back into the pot with water along with the bread crumbs and 8 oz of evaporated milk and bring to boil and then reduce the heat to maintain a simmer for 15 minutes, stirring to get a semi thick sauce.

7. Stir the ground walnuts and parmesan into the pot and allow to simmer for another 3 to 5 minutes. At this point season with salt and pepper to taste.

8. Now it is ready to be served with a portion of rice. Typical Peruvian garnishes include pitted

black olives and slices of hard boil egg, although neither is required to enjoy this dish.

Seco de Res

Seco de Res in Peru is a fantastic cilantro beef stew. It is a criolla dish that can be served with almost any accompanying dish, although, I would recommend it with either rice or potatoes cooked however you like them best. The accompanying dish will not be included in this recipe, so take note and prepare that to be ready for when you have finished preparing this dish.

Ingredients for 6 good servings

- 2 lbs. (0.9 Kg) beef

- 2 cups beef stock

- 1 large potato

- 1 Onion

- 3 Garlic cloves

- Half a cup green peas

- 1 Carrot

- 1 tsp. ground cumin

- 1 tbsp. Vegetable oil

- 1 tbsp. aji paste

- 1 tbsp. cilantro

- 1 cup water
- Salt and Pepper

Preparation - 2 hours

1. Finely chop the onion, crush the 3 garlic cloves, chop up 1 carrot, peel and cube the large potato, and also cut the beef up into cubes about the size of you thumb.

2. With a little bit of water blend the 1 tbsp. of cilantro.

3. Using a small bowl, mix the now crushed garlic, the 1 tsp. of ground cumin and a pinch of salt and pepper.

4. Using a large bowl, put in all of the cubed beef and pour the contents of the small bowl over the beef and mix them together thoroughly.

5. Cover the bowl and leave to marinate for one hour or longer.

6. Using a large pan, heat some vegetable oil in the bottom on a medium heat.

7. When the oil is hot, add the marinated beef and cook until the meat is brown and sealed on all sides.

8. Add the finely chopped onion, the blended cilantro and the 1 tsp. of aji paste. Stir whilst cooking until the meat is soft, and then add in the 2 cups of beef stock.

9.	With the beef stock added, bring the to boil and then reduce to a simmer and cook for 20 minutes. Be sure to stir from time to time.

10.	Add the cubed potatoes with the cup of water and cook until the potatoes are tender. This will typically take 15 to 20 minutes.

11.	Add the half cup of green peas and the chopped carrot and cook for a further 5 to 10 minutes until the carrot is soft.

12.	And finally, you have Seco de Res ready to serve on a plate with rice and, or potatoes. Delicious!

Tacu Tacu

Maybe not the healthiest thing to do with beans and rice is to fry them, but this is such a tasty dish that it could not go missed in this book.

Ingredients for 4 servings

- 2 cups beans, ideally borloti

- 2 oz. (56 grams) bacon

- 1 red onion

- 6 garlic cloves

- 2 tsp. ají chili

- 1 cup rice

- 6 tbsp. olive oil

- 4 tsp. dried oregano

- Salt and pepper

Preparation - 12 hours+

1. Soak the 2 cups of beans in water and leave overnight. The beans will need to soak for at least 10 hours.

2. After the beans have been allowed to soak drain any remaining water and rinse the beans.

3.   Fill a large pot with water, bring it to the boil and then place the soaked beans into the boiling water. Reduce the heat as required to maintain a simmer.

4.   Cut the bacon into small pieces and add them to the pot with the beans, continuing to simmer until the beans become very soft.

5.   Whilst the beans and bacon are cooking use this time to mince the onion and the 6 garlic cloves.

6.   Using a large pan or wok on a low heat add 1 tbsp. of olive.

7.   When the oil is hot, put in half of the minced onion, half of the minced garlic and 1 tbsp. of chili. Cook this for 10 to 15 minutes. Put this to one side, it will be needed later. (See step 11)

8.   In a different pot heat 1 tbsp. of oil on a low heat and then when the oil is hot, put in the other half of the minced garlic and cook until just browned.

9.   Add the cup of rice to this pot and stir the garlic oil over all the rice and cook for no more than 2 minutes.

10.   Add in 2 cups of water, and 1 tsp. (if desired, tastes good with the salt also). Bring to the boil, cover the pot and then reduce the heat to maintain a simmer until the rice is completely cooked.

11.   When the beans have cooked and they are completely soft add the saved (From step 7) onion garlic mixture and season with a pinch of

salt and pepper.

12.   Combine and mix together the contents of both pots.

13.   In a wok add some oil and heat over a low to medium heat. When the oil is hot add a quarter of the remaining minced onion and 1 tsp. of oregano and saute until the onion is soft and slightly brown.

14.   Take a quarter of the bean rice mixture and form the shape of an American football. Place this football in the wok and cook so that it forms a brown base.

15.   Flip, or turn the football over in the wok so that the other side also cooks.

16.   When the football has a nice brown crust all over then it is ready to be served.

17.   Follow this for the other 3 quarters of the onion and the bean rice mixture.

18.   The Tacu Tacu is now ready to be served. It goes very well with Chicharrones.

Arroz con Pato

This fantastic duck and rice dish originally comes from the northern coast of Peru. You can change the duck for chicken in this dish, but frankly the duck comes out so good that you are not going to want to do that.

Ingredients for 4 servings

- 2.5 lbs. (1.35 Kg) Duck
- 1 Onion
- 1 Bell pepper
- 3 Garlic cloves
- 2 cups of Rice
- 2 cups of dark Beer
- 2 cups water
- Quarter cup of Oil
- 1 bunch of Cilantro
- Salt and pepper

Preparation - 90 minutes+

1. Both the onion and bell pepper need to be finely chopped, mince the 3 garlic cloves and

then finely chop up the bunch of cilantro.

2.   Cut the duck up into quarters more or less, you want to have 4 fairly equally sized pieces. Do not remove the skin.

3.   Using a fork, prick the skin of the duck pieces.

4.   With a large pan heat the oil with a medium-high heat.

5.   With one to two pieces of duck at a time, put them in the pan with the hot oil and brown on both sides before removing and placing on a plate to the side for later.

6.   Remove any excess oil from the pan, so that you have enough oil to saute the onion and pepper, which is what needs to be done next.

7.   After 5 minutes, add the minced garlic to the pan with the onion and pepper and saute for a further 2 to 3 minutes.

8.   Using a blender add 1 cup of water and the finely chopped cilantro and blend into a puree.

9.   Add the duck pieces back to the large pan that contains the onion, pepper etc... along with the cilantro puree, 1 cup of water and 2 cups of dark beer (1 bottle is fine).

10.   Bring all this to the boil then reduce the heat to allow to simmer for 30 minutes. The duck should be tender before the next step.

11.   Add to the pan the 2 cups of rice and make sure that the water is at a simmer, and cover the pot and cook for approximately 15 minutes.

12. When the rice is cooked, remove the pan from the heat and leave to rest for 5 minutes, after which you can fluff the rice using a fork.

13. And now it is ready to serve. Place the pieces of duck over a bed of rice on each plate.

Pollo a la Brasa

This is rotisserie chicken Peruvian style. It is very popular in Peru and really it is an easy and tasty dish to make. Note that you will probably have to prepare the marinade the day before and that is served with French fries and a small side salad. Neither the French fries nor the side salad are included in this recipe so prepare them as you desire.

Ingredients for 4 servings

- 1 whole chicken quartered

- 6 garlic cloves

- Third of a cup soy sauce

- 2 tbsp. fresh lime juice

- 2 tsp. ground cumin

- 1 tsp. ground aji chili (or paprika)

- Half tsp. dried oregano

- 1 tbsp. vegetable oil

Preparation - 12 hours +

1. First, you will need to prepare the marinade for the chicken.

2. Put the 2 tbsp. of lime juice, the 1 tsp. of ground aji chili (or paprika), the half tsp. of oregano, the soy sauce, the cumin and the 6 peeled garlic cloves all into a blender with a little oil.

3. Blend this together for 5 minutes.

4. Cut the whole chicken up in quarters after having removed the innards.

5. Place the chicken in an airtight container with the marinade and leave in a refrigerator for 12 to 24 hours. Note, plastic freezer bags also work very well for this purpose.

6. After the chicken has marinated light the grill up to a medium-high heat.

7. Remove the chicken from the marinade and pat it dry of the marinade.

8. Oil or grease the grill rack and then place then chicken on to it.

9. Start off grilling the skin side of the chicken first, note that you don't want the heat from the coals or a burner directly at the chicken, remove some of the coals or knock out one of the gas burners to achieve this.

10. After about 15 minutes turn the chicken over and cook for a further 15 to 20 minutes on the other side until the chicken is completely cooked.

11. Serve with French fries and a small side salad.

Chicharrones

This really is a very simple recipe and these go great with a Tacu Tacu and some aji sauce. These are fried pieces of pork that could equally be cooked as a starter or a snack. Surprising delicious for such a simple dish.

Ingredients for 6 servings

* 4 lbs. (1.8 Kg) pork belly

* 4 garlic cloves

* 2 tbsp. of salt

* 1 Quart (1 liter) of water

Preparation - 2 hours+

1) Cut the 4 lbs. of pork into pieces of approximately 2 to 3 inches each, making sure to leave the fat and bone on the pieces.

2) Using a large pan, put in the 2 tbsp. of salt, the 4 garlic cloves and the now chopped up pork belly.

3) Add the water and bring to the boil. After which reduce the heat to maintain a simmer until all of the water has be cooked away.

4) Now allow the pork to fry in its own fat until a

golden brown layer has formed on the pork. It should also be crispy.

5) The Chicharrones are now ready to be served. If they are a little greasy then dry them first in paper towel before serving.

Octopus in Olive Sauce

This is a super easy to make octopus dish that will be sure to impress your family and friends. This dish can be used as a main course, a starter or snack. Simple, quick and delicious, what more can you ask for?

Ingredients for 4 servings

- 3 lb. (1.35 kg) octopus

- 16 black pitted olives

- 3 tbsp. lime juice

- 2 cups olive oil

- 2 tbsp. parsley

- 2 Eggs

- Salt and Pepper

- 3 tbsp. olive oil for decoration

Preparation - 1 hour

1. Boil a large pot of water and then add the octopus so that it is completely submerged underneath the water. Place a cover and boil for 35 to 40 minutes, so that the octopus is soft.

2. When the octopus is soft remove from the heat

and from the pot. Remove the dark skin from the octopus.

3.   Next, to make the mayonnaise, in a bowl or blender, beat or blend the eggs into a pinch of salt, a pinch of pepper and the 2 cups of lime juice. Gradually blend in the olive oil until a thick mayonnaise is created.

4.   Now, you will need to take half of the mayonnaise and put to one side before adding the pitted olives to the blender.

5.   Blend the olives into the mayonnaise until you have obtained a thick puree. Now mix in the half of the mayonnaise that you had put to one side.

6.   Cut the octopus up into slices and put them into a dish, which can be covered with the olive mayonnaise sauce.

7.   To garnish, mince the parsley and sprinkle over the top of the dish along with the 3 tbsp. of olive oil.

Pescado Sudado

Pescado Sudado is quite simply Peruvian steamed fish fillets. This is a very tasty, quick, easy and healthy dish to make. Please note that the accompaniment of either rice or potatoes is not included in this recipe and you will need to prepare that accordingly based on your preferences.

Ingredients for 4 servings

- 1.5 lbs. (0.68 Kg) of flounder or sole fillets

- 2 tomatoes

- 1 onion

- 2 garlic cloves

- 2 tbsp. olive oil

- Half tsp. of aji chili (or paprika)

- Half cup dry white wine

- 12 sprigs fresh parsley, leaves only, chopped

- 1 Lemon

- Salt

Preparation - 25 minutes

1. Finely chop up the 2 tomatoes, cut the onion into thin half moon shapes and finely chop up the 2 garlic cloves.

2. Next using a large skillet, add the olive oil and heat with a low-medium heat.

3. Now, with the oil hot, add in the finely chopped onion, tomatoes, garlic, the half tsp. of aji or ground paprika and a pinch of salt.

4. Stir-fry all this for 5 minutes. The onion should have turned a very light brown.

5. Place the flounder or sole fillets on top of the stir-fry in the skillet, covering it all with the half cup of dry white wine.

6. Cook for a further 5 minutes until the fish is cooked. Whilst this is ongoing, finely chop up the parsley and cut the lemon into quarters.

7. The dish is now ready to be served with either rice or potatoes. Garnish the fish with the chopped parsley and place a quarter lemon on each plate.

Causa de Pollo

This Peruvian classic is like a cake that make up of potato, avocado and chicken. It is served cold and is truly delicious.

Note, the chicken can be substituted with tuna or crab, either work very well.

Ingredients for 4 servings

- 2 Chicken breasts
- 2 Avocado
- 4 Potatoes
- 2 Shallots
- 2 Eggs
- 4 aji peppers
- Half a cup Sugar
- Quarter cup vinegar
- 4 tbsp. Vegetable oil
- 2 tsp. Cumin
- 1 Cup Chicken stock
- 2 Cup Mayonnaise
- 2 Cup Corn kernels

- 4 tbsp. Cilantro

- 2 tbsp. Orange juice

- 2 Lime juiced

- 4 Large lettuce leaves

- Salt and Pepper

Preparation - 2 hours

There are three distinct phases to preparing this dish, first you need to prepare the potato puree, then the filling and then finally you need to assemble it all together.

Potato Puree

1. Peel and then cut the 4 potatoes into small pieces. Place them in a pot of water with a pinch of salt and bring this to the boil until the potatoes are cooked.

2. Seed and vein the 4 yellow peppers. Put them in a pot of water and bring to the boil. Reduce the heat and allow to simmer until the peppers are soft. This will take approximately half an hour.

3. Finely chop up the 2 shallots and place in a small bowl with a pinch of salt and the quarter cup of vinegar and let marinate.

4. Strain the marinated shallots and put into a blender with the half cup of sugar with a splash

of oil and vinegar. Blend this all together.

5.	Puree the now cooked potatoes in the blender with the marinade and then add the lime juice, the yellow peppers and the shallots that have been left in the vinegar for at least 30 minutes and a pinch of salt.

6.	Mix all of this together.

7.	Now, you will need to cook the 2 cups of corn kernels until soft and then drain them.

8.	In a separate bowl mix the cooked corn kernels with 3 tbsp. of orange juice. Chop up 4 tbsp. of cilantro and add this with a pinch of salt and pepper. Save this separately.

Filling

1.	In a skillet heat some oil and cook the chicken breast until it is completely sealed.

2.	Add in the chicken stock and cumin, bring to boil and then reduce the heat to a simmer and cook until the chicken is tender but cooked.

3.	Let the chicken cool until it can be handled and then shred it. Note, you can also do thing in a food processor.

4.	Season the shredded chicken with salt and pepper.

Putting it all together

1. Take a ring mold and oil and line it.

2. Spread a layer of the puree potato mixture across the bottom of the mold, approximately half an inch to an inch thick. Flatten and smooth using the back of a teaspoon.

3. On top of the potato spread a thin layer of mayonnaise.

4. Place in the mixture of corn kernels pressing down on them to form a even layer.

5. Place another layer of potato puree and flatten again, top this with another thin layer of mayonnaise.

6. Now cut the avocado into thin slices and place them on top of the mayonnaise followed by another layer of potato puree.

7. Put on a layer of the shredded chicken and then spread a thin layer of mayonnaise on top of the chicken, follow this with a final thin layer of potato puree.

8. This now needs to be placed in the refrigerator for a least one hour, during which time you need to hard-boil the two eggs and then cut them into small pieces when they have cooled.

9. Serve on a bed of lettuce and place the cut up hard-boiled egg pieces on top.

Goat Stew

Traditionally this is a goat stew, but it works equally as well substituting the goat for lamb. This great dish originates from the Andes, it is normally served with rice or potatoes, neither of which have been included in this recipe so you will need to prepare them also.

Note, Chicha de Jora may be difficult to obtain, but a sweet white wine or sherry are reasonable substitutes.

Ingredients for 4 servings

- 1.5 lbs. goat meat
- 2 Red onions
- 8 Garlic cloves
- 1 bunch of scallions
- 1 bunch of cilantro
- Half cup of vinegar
- 1 Cup of Chicha de Jora
- 1 tbsp. ground Ají chili (cayenne if not aji not available)
- Quarter Cup of Vegetable or olive oil
- Salt and Pepper

Preparation - 2 hours+

1. Cut the goat meat into pieces of about 4 oz. each and put them and the vinegar together in a bowl making sure that the vinegar is rubbed into the meat. Leave to marinate for at least one hour.

2. Whilst the goat meat is marinating, chop up the 2 onions, they do not need to be finely chopped. Also, chop up the bunch of scallions and the bunch of cilantro.

3. Using a Dutch oven, or pot on the stove, heat the oil in with a medium-high heat and when hot place in the now marinated goat pieces. Saute the goat meat until there is very little liquid remaining in the pot.

4. Using a blender, mix the garlic cloves with the cilantro and chicha de jora (or sweet white wine or sherry).

5. Add this mixture into the pot containing the goat meat. Also add the chopped onion, the aji chili and the chopped scallions.

6. Cover the pot and maintain the liquid at a simmer for approximately 1 hour, depending on the size of the goat pieces. Obviously, you may need a little more time if they are large or a little less time if they are small.

7. Before serving, add salt and pepper to taste.

8. Serve with either rice or potatoes cooked however you prefer.

Pot Roast

In Peru this is called Asado de Res and is served with mashed potatoes or mashed sweet potatoes, but boiled potatoes work equally well. Please note that this recipe does not include how to prepare the potatoes and you will have to plan that accordingly.

Ingredients for 6 servings

- 4 lbs. (3.5 Kg) boneless round tip roast
- 15 oz. (425 grams) tomato sauce (1 can)
- 12 Garlic cloves
- 1 Onion
- 1 tsp. cumin seed
- 2 tsp. salt, divided
- 2 tsp. black pepper
- 2 tbsp. of corn starch
- Quarter cup vegetable oil
- 1.5 cups red wine
- Water

Preparation - 2 hours 30 minutes

1. Chop the onion into thick slices.

2. Mince the 12 garlic cloves and put them in a bowl with the 1 tsp. of cumin seeds, a pinch of salt and pepper and then mix together well until a paste is formed.

3. Cut approximately one inch deep slices into the piece of meat and stuff with the garlic paste.

4. Use a large pot to heat the oil, then place the meat into the pot and cook to seal the meat on all sides.

5. When the meat has browned, add the 15 oz. of tomato sauce, the 1.5 cups of red wine and enough water so that half of the meat is submerged and the other half above the liquid.

6. Add a pinch of salt and pepper and the chopped onion, and then stir well all the liquid.

7. Cover the pot, bring to the boil and then reduce the heat to a steady simmer.

8. Every 15 minutes turn the roast over. Continue this for 2 hours and verify the meat is cooked.

9. Thoroughly mix the 2 tbsp. of corn starch with water. Then using juices from the pot use this to serve as gravy.

10. When the meat is cooked, cut into slices to serve with the gravy and potatoes or sweet potatoes, either mashed or boiled.

Fish Ceviche

This is one of the most famous dishes from Peru, it is raw fish marinated in spiced lime juice. This dish is typically served with cooked corn kernels and a couple of slices of sweet potato and a lettuce leaf. None of the accompaniments have been included in this recipe and you will need to prepare them as you desire. Note, this dish is still delicious without the accompaniments.

Ingredients for 6 Servings

- 2 lbs. (0.9 Kg) of Flounder or sole filets
- 2 Red onions
- 4 Ají Chili's
- 2 Garlic cloves
- 1 cup lime juice
- 1 bunch of parsley
- 2 Lemons
- 1 tsp. salt
- Half tsp. pepper

Preparation - 1 hour 30 minutes

1. Finely chop up the 2 onions into thin half

moons, crush the 2 garlic cloves and seed, vane and very thinly cut the 4 aji peppers into slices.

2. Carefully remove both the skin and all of the bones from the fish fillets. It is important to make sure that there are no bones remaining.

3. Cut the fish fillets into small bite size pieces.

4. Place all of the ingredients together into a large bowl and mix thoroughly together.

5. Place the bowl into the refrigerator for 1 hour and allow to marinate.

6. Cut the lemon in quarters.

7. Remove the bowl from the refrigerator and stir a couple of times before serving.

8. Mince the parsley and sprinkle over the top of the ceviche.

9. Serve with corn, camote (sweet potato) and a lettuce leaf, plus a quarter piece of lemon.

Scallop Ceviche

This is another Ceviche variation, except this time using scallops instead of fish. This recipe is a little spicy, so be warned.

Ingredients for 4 servings

- 1 lb. (0.45 Kg) Scallops

- 2 onion minced

- 1 Rocoto pepper

- 3 Garlic cloves

- 2 tbsp. sesame seed oil

- 2 tbsp. sesame seeds

- Juice of 6 limes

- 1 tsp. salt

- 1 tsp. sugar

- Half tsp. ground pepper

- 4 sprigs of Parsley

- 1 small avocado

- 2 Limes

Preparation - 1 hour 30 minutes

1.   Mince the 2 onions, mince the recoto pepper, mince the 3 garlic cloves and then wash the scallops before cutting them up into small pieces.

2.   Put all of the ingredients together in a large bowl and stir them together thoroughly.

3.   Place the bowl in a refrigerator for at least 1 hour to allow the mixture to marinate.

4.   Before serving, cut the ripe avocado into 8 equal slices, finely chop up the parsley, and chop in half each of the 2 limes.

5.   Serve the ceviche in bowls sprinkling some parsley over each, then place a couple of piece of avocado on top and a piece lime on the side.

Desserts

There are literally so many great desserts to choose from in Peru it was hard to select only a few. However, although the list here is not very big, here are some fantastic examples of Peruvian desserts.

Tres Leches

Tres Leches translates as three milks in English, and this is exactly that, a desert with of three milks. The name conjures up images of something akin to rice pudding, which is not was this is. Tres leches is a cake comprising of three layers, cream on top of a flan type cake which is sat in milk. Very simple yet delicious.

Ingredients for 8 to 10 servings

- 5 Eggs

- 1.5 cups all purpose flour

- 1.5 tsp. baking powder

- 1 cup sugar

- 4 oz. Whole milk

- 4 oz. (120 ml) condensed milk (sweetened)

- 4 oz. (120 ml) evaporated milk

- 10 oz. Thick cream

- 2.5 tsp. vanilla essence

- 3 tbsp. of olive oil

- 3 tsp. of ground cinnamon

Preparation - 3 hours+

1. Set the oven on to 350 F (177 C, or gas mark 3) and let it preheat.

2. Now use a large bowl and sift the flour into the bowl, adding the baking powder and a pinch of salt. Mix them together thoroughly.

3. Using a separate bowl, break the 5 eggs into the bowl and beat until their size is 2 to 3 times bigger and then add 1 cup of sugar in bit by bit followed by 1 tsp. of vanilla extract continuing to beat the eggs. Now, gently add and stir in 3 tbsp. of olive oil and 4 oz. of whole milk. All this can be done in a food processor.

4. Maintain the blender on a low speed and add the flour mixture into the egg mixture slowly. Attempt to keep the frothy texture of the mixture whilst doing this.

5. Grease a baking tray (ideally a Pyrex 8 by 12 inch tray, which is 20 by 30 cm), and pour the mixture into the tray.

6. Place the tray into the now hot oven for 30 to 35 minutes.

7. After the 30 to 35 minutes, remove the tray from the oven and place on the top, leaving in the tray and allowing it to cool to approximately ambient temperature.

8. After the cake has cooled use a fork or skewer to prick all the way over.

9. Time to prepare the milk mixture. For this use

the 4 oz. of evaporated milk, 4 oz. of condensed milk (sweetened) and 4 oz. of thick cream.

10.   Thoroughly mix all three of these in a bowl.

11.   Pour the milk mixture over the cake that is still in the tray. The cake will soak up all of the milk.

12.   Cover the cake and place in the refrigerator for a minimum of 2 hours, ideally 5 or 6 hours, or until the majority of the milk mixture has been absorbed by the cake.

13.   Shortly before serving the cake you will need to make the topping. Using a food processor mix together 6 oz. of thick cream, 1.5 tsp. of vanilla extract and 1 tbsp. of fine white sugar. Continue to mix until the cream forms stiff peaks.

14.   Cover the cake with the whipped cream and then sprinkle on top 3 tsp. of cinnamon.

15.   The cake can now be cut and served. It can be kept in a refrigerator for up to one day.

Picarones with Syrup

This is without a doubt one of the most popular deserts in Peru. Picarones are very addictive, and often sold on the street from venders or in parks and even in restaurants. These are round donut shaped fried squash rings. They are served with their own syrup, which is included in this recipe.

Ingredients for 6 servings

- 1 lb. (0.45 Kg) Squash

- 1 lb. (0.45 Kg) Sweet potato

- 1 lb. (0.45 Kg) flour

- 3 tbsp. yeast

- 4 Cinnamon sticks

- 8 cloves

- 2 tsp. anise seeds

- 2 oz. of molasses

- 3 tbsp. sugar

- 2 Eggs

- Vegetable Oil as needed

- 1 cup white sugar

- 1 Orange

- 2 Limes

- 4 cups water

Preparation - 3 hours

This recipe is divided into the two components to make it clearer to follow. First the picarones, and then the syrup.

Picarones

1. Fill a large pot with water and bring to the boil. Place 2 of the cinnamon sticks, the 2 tsp. of anise and 4 cloves in a pot. Maintain the water boiling for 10 minutes.

2. Whilst the water is boiling, use this time to peel the squash and sweet potatoes and cut them both into large pieces.

3. After 10 minutes, strain the water and use the same water for boiling the sweet potatoes and squash in. Cook the potatoes and squash until soft.

4. When cooked, remove both the potatoes and squash and mash them together to form a puree, then allow it to cool.

5. Note, do not through away the cooking water, keep 2 cups worth.

6. With these two cups of water, mix them with

the 3 tbsp. yeast and cup of sugar and let stand for 10 minutes.

7. Add the squash and potato puree, the 2 eggs and a pinch of salt to the yeast mixture and mix well.

8. Now gradually add in the flour to the mixture and mix continually until the dough is smooth, stretchy and only a little bit sticky.

9. Cover the bowl with a damp cloth on top and let stand for 2 hours or until the dough has doubled in size.

10. Fill a large pan with oil and heat to approximately 350 F (177 C).

11. Using your fingers, form thin donut shapes from the dough. Toss these into the hot oil, turn over after 20 to 30 seconds, then after one minute remove the fried rings. The donut shapes should be a golden brown on both sides before removing and placing them on a plate covered with paper towel.

12. These are the picarones, they are now ready to eat.

Syrup

1. This can be prepared whilst the dough is rising.

2. Remove the rinds from the limes and the orange, then squeeze the juice from them.

3. Put this juice in a pot with the rinds. Also, add 3

tbsp. of sugar, 2 oz. of molasses, the remaining 2 cinnamon sticks, 4 cloves and half a cup of water. Bring this all to the boil whilst stirring continually.

4.   Reduce the heat and allow to simmer for 10 to 15 minutes until the syrup has thicken a little.

5.   Strain the rinds and spices from the syrup and it is ready to be drizzled over a couple of picarones.

Sweet Potato Flan

In Peru this is called Flan de Camote, and this is a delicious yet very simple dessert to make. If possible use the camote sweet potato from Peru. Failing that almost any sweet potato will do as a substitute.

Ingredients for 8 serving flan

- 2 lbs. (0.9Kg) sweet potato

- 16 oz. (473 ml) of evaporated milk

- 8 oz. (226 grams) wheat flour

- 3 cups of sugar

- 2 large eggs

- 3 tbsp. butter

- 3 tbsp. vanilla extract

- Slivered almonds

Preparation - 2 hours

1. Peel the 2 lbs. of sweet potato, then boil, and then mash them. This will take approximately 20 minutes.

2. When this is complete, preheat oven to 350 F (177 C, or gas mark 3).

3. Using a large bowl, mix the flour, milk and mashed sweet potato together until it is smooth without any lumps.

4. In a small pan or in the microwave melt the 2 tbsp. of butter. Add the melted butter to the mixture.

5. Add the 3 cups of sugar, the 2 large eggs and the 3 tbsp. of vanilla extract, mixing as they are added.

6. Grease a pie dish, and then add the mixture.

7. Put this dish into the oven for 30 to 40 minutes, baking until firm.

8. Remove the dish from the oven and let cool for at least 30 minutes.

9. Cut up the slivered almonds and sprinkle on top of the flan.

10. It is now ready to be served.

11. Note, this can be keep for up to a couple of days in the refrigerator.

Drinks

Here we have a very small but select trio of Peruvian drinks. The first of which is non-alcoholic and the second two are pretty potent alcoholic beverages, so be warned.

No meal in Peru would be complete without at least having one of these drinks to accompany your food.

Note, if Peruvian limes are not available then key limes tend to make a very good substitute.

Chicha Morada

One of the most common sights you will see on any table in any restaurant or home in Peru is this dark red corn based non-alcoholic drink, which accompanies almost every meal. This drink can actually be traced all the way back to the Inca's. Something else to note is that this is a drink that can be served warm or cold depending on your mood and or the climate at the time.

Ingredients for 8 glasses

- 1 lb. (0.5 Kg) or red/purple corn (dried)

- 1.5 (5.7 l) Gallons of Water

- The rind from one pineapple

- 1.5 cups of sugar

- 2 Cinnamon sticks

- Juice from 1 lime

Preparation - 4 hours+

1. You will need a large pot or saucepan for this. Put all the corn, the pineapple rind, and the cinnamon sticks into the large pot or saucepan.

2. Pour all the water over the top, place the lid on the pot and then put the heat on high.

3.   When the juice begins to boil it is time to turn the heat down to a gentle simmer.

4.   After 60 minutes of simmering, remove the lid from the pot and allow the liquid to reduce a little. Do this for approximately 30 minutes.

5.   The liquid should now be very dark. At which point it is time to remove the heat and allow the liquid to cool for 2 to 3 hours.

6.   When the liquid is cool, it is time to get separate the liquid from the corn, pineapple and cinnamon. To do this use a colander and discard everything from the pot expect for the liquid.

7.   Add the lime juice and sugar and stir into the liquid. You can add or reduce the sugar depending on your taste. As such I would only add half of the sugar initially, and add the rest to suite.

8.   It is now possible to drink and enjoy the Chicha Morada or as most people prefer it cold you can put in the fridge for 2 to 3 hours, then enjoy it.

Pisco Sour

If there is one drink that Peru is famous for, this is it. The origins of Pisco remained disputed between Peru and Chile, but the bottom line is this is a fantastic drink that carries more punch that you realize. The main ingredient is Pisco, which is a grape based brandy, taken from the grapes in the Peruvian and Chilean vineyards.

Ingredients to make 4 drinks

- 12 oz. (340 ml) of Pisco
- A handful of Ice Cubes
- 4 oz. (113 ml) of Lime Juice
- 1 Egg White
- 4 oz. (113 ml) Sugar Syrup (Goma de Jarabe is the choice in Peru)
- A few drops of Aromatic Bitter (Angostura Bitter)
- Fine White Sugar (optional)

Preparation - 10 minutes

1. Note, with a blender Pisco Sour is an easy drink to make.

2. Put the Pisco with a handful of ice cubes, the

sugar syrup and the lime juice into a blender. Note that the longest part of making this drink can be squeezing the limes.

3.   Add the white of one egg to this mixture.

4.   Blend the mixture for several minutes. What you want to do is to make sure all the ice has been crushed. By the time you are finished the mixture will look like foam.

5.   At this point you should test the mix for taste, if it is too bitter or acidic then add some of the sugar, teaspoon at a time and blend the mixture again. Do this until you the drink is as you like it. Personally I never add sugar. I find that the sugar syrup is sweet enough.

6.   The drink is now ready to be poured into glasses. Add a drop or two of the aromatic bitter in the center of the glass after the drink has been poured.

7.   It will take at 10 minutes or so for the drink to settle and for the foam to settle on the top of the glass. However, you can go ahead and enjoy this drink before it has settled.

Chilcano

This is possibly one of the easiest drinks to make. It is a refreshing long drink, great for anytime of the afternoon or evening. Unlike Pisco Sour, which can sometimes feel a bit to acidic, Chilcano is a very smooth drink. Perfect for a spring or summer evening.

Ingredients for 4 drinks

*   8 oz. (227 ml) Pisco

*   16 oz. (452 ml) Ginger Ale

*   A handful of Ice cubes

*   Juice from 1 lime

Preparation - 2 minutes

1. Fill 4 tall tumbler glasses with ice cubes.

2. Pour the Pisco over the ice cubes, 2 oz. in each of the 4 glasses.

3. Splash some of the squeezed lime juice into each glass.

4. Finally top off each glass with the ginger ale.

5. And bingo you have yourself 4 Chilcanos!

6. For an added touch you can cut a slice of lime and place it into each glass. This drink is often

drunk with a straw.

Also by this Author

Firstly, thank you for purchasing this book, and I hope you enjoyed the recipes.

Should you have an interest in Spanish or ever have the opportunity to travel to Peru, you may also be interested in the following book about the slang used in Peru.

¿Quién me llama? Learn Peruvian Spanish Slang

Don't get caught out in Peru by not knowing at least a little of the local Spanish slang.

In this book, the most important slang words that are spoken day to day on the streets in Peru are explained in English. As an added bonus each word comes with a sample sentence in Spanish to help contextualise the use of each word.

The contents of this book will give you some important slang words and phrases that will make your time in Peru that much more enjoyable.

Don't go to Peru without a copy of this book.

Available at amazon.com

Made in the USA
San Bernardino, CA
17 July 2013